Unit

Changes Over Time

Contents

Dave Was Late

Why was Dave late?
Dave had a way to get up.
Dave set a clock when
he went to bed, but the
bell didn't ring.

2

Now Dave rushed and ate.
Then, Dave had to bake
some cakes. Dave had to
shake and shake. He mixed
and mixed.

Dave baked six cakes.
He set them on a rack.
Then, Dave set a cake on
a plate. Dave set the rest
in a safe place.

Dave had to take his hat.
Dave dashed up Grape
Lane. Dave ran up to a
bus stop. The bus just
rushed away.

Dave was late for his job today. Dave had to make ten cakes at Jane's Bake Shop!

Is It Late?

Is he late for a game?
Check a clock! Why? A
clock will tell when it is
late and when it is not late.

Is Kate late for a date
with Jane? No. Kate can
wake up now. Kate will
have fun today!

Am I late for a snack? No.
Take a bunch of grapes.
Place some on a plate.
Take the rest away.

Is Tim late for the bus? No.
Tim and dad make it to the
bus. Tim is not late!
Which way will Tim go?

Eliza Snow/E+/Getty Images, (inset) Ingram Publishing

Is Blake late for the race?
No. Blake can chase Rick.
Blake can run fast. She
can win the match!

A Fine Plant

MIKE

PLANT

JANE

"Let us make this bud
   grow together," said Jane.
"Yes! It will be fun,"
said Mike.
"I bet it will get big!"

"I can tip a water can,"
said Mike. "Then it should
get big."
"That is nice!" said Plant.

"This bud can chat!"
said Mike.
"Yes! I like it in the sun. It
will make me smile and rise
up," said Plant.

"This plant is not a pine. It is not a vine," said Jane.
"Now I am a pretty pink plant with a green stem," said Plant.

"This plant did get big. It did take time," said Mike.
"I will not stop while I get sun and water," said Plant.

18

Plants Take Time to Grow

Plants can be green.
Plants can be a big size.
Plants can be pretty.
They can grow in a lot
of ways.

It takes time to grow a plant. To make a plant grow, you should add some water. Plants like to get wet.

Place it in a fine spot with sun. Plants like the sun to shine on them. The sun will make plants rise.

A pine is a plant. A pine
can rise up to a big size.
Pines can grow together in
a line. They take time to
grow.

A plant is a fine thing.
When a plant has time,
it can rise and grow big.
A plant can make life good!

King and Five Mice

Once upon a time, a cat had the name of King. King had a space to rest. It was at the edge of the green grass.

Then, five mice went on top of King's face. It did wake him up. King made a face that was not so happy.

King was in a rage. He
had the mice in a cage.
The five mice said, "Let us
out. We can help."

28

King did ask, "Can mice help
me? I will take a chance."
The five mice ran fast from
that cage!

Then on a hunt, King got in
a net. He could not budge in
any way. The five mice came
and bit the net. King got out!
Such fine mice!

Tales from a Past Age

At times, a tale said "Once upon a time." A tale like this comes from a past age. Can you name a tale?

andresr/E+/Getty Images, (inset) McGraw-Hill Education

A tale like this can have
things that are made up.
It can have mice that sing.
It can have pigs that use
bricks.

In a tale like this, the two pals go to new places. They can get a gem. They can have a race.

(tl) David H. Collier/Stockbyte/Getty Images, (b) S953554/iStock/Getty Images, (tr) mstay/Digital Vision Vectors/Getty Images

In a tale like this, a plant can sit on a ledge. A king can be on a bridge. A bug can end up in a cage.

A tale like this can end in a happy way. The faces can have smiles! So look at a tale from any past age. It will be fun!

Those Old Classes

Long ago, a school was not like it is now. It had a huge bell. That bell rang a tone. It was time for class!

A school sat in a lone spot.
A boy had a desk. A girl had
a desk. Desks had quill pens.
Quill pens used black ink.
People could use these quills
to write notes.

Today boys and girls use a globe in school. Long ago they used a globe to find lakes and lands. A globe is like a map. You can find many things on a globe.

How did girls and boys get to class then? They walked a lot. Did they pledge to the flag? Yes!

An old class is not quite
the same as now. But one
thing is the same. They still
have fun in class!

That Old Globe

Eve and Pete like old things
from long ago. This time,
Pete had an old globe.
Eve said, "Let's use this."

Eve spun that globe, and they did not end up at home!
Pete looked and there was a note. It was a time in the past.

Eve and Pete land in a
huge place with a lot of
crops.
Eve said, "These people
use a mule. It is not like at
home."

In a lodge, Pete said, "How can they make things to eat?"

"This boy and girl get it from the pot on that stove," said Eve.

Eve spun the globe again.
Eve and Pete came back
home!
They said, "The past is not
like now. But it was fun!"

A Good Cook

When a cook makes a dish,
she likes to use fresh things.
Every dish must look good.
It must taste good, too.

A good cook can get a
ripe lime. A ship will bring
limes in a box. After that
a cook will buy them.

A good cook can make
bread. He will push and
pull it. Soon he will bake
it. When it is done, it will
make a fine bite!

A good cook can use fish.
A man must put a hook
on a pole to get a fish.
Then a cook will buy a
fish. She will put it in a pan.

It is a lot of work to be a cook. A good cook can get a lot of help. If a cook makes a good dish, then people will say, "Yum!"

That Looks Good

Rose and Chad liked
to cook. Every time they
cooked, they placed good
things in a pot. When it
was done, Rose and Chad
ate those good things up.

Soon, they did not have
much. Rose and Chad had
to shop.
"What can we buy?" asked
Chad.
"We can take a look," said
Rose.

Gene is a bull that works
in the shop. Rose could see
him grab and pull a big
lump. Then, Gene made
it flat.

"What is that?" asked Rose.
"Pizza," said Gene with
a big smile.
He set the dish on wood.
Gene set it in a hot spot.

After a bit of time, Gene
took the dish out.
"Yum. That smells so good."
said Rose and Chad with
big smiles.

Dave Was Late

DECODABLE WORDS
Target Phonics Elements
  Long *a, a_e:* ate, bake, cake, cakes,
  Dave, Grape, Jane's, lane, late,
  make, plate, safe, take

HIGH-FREQUENCY WORDS
away, now, some, today, way,
why
Review: eat, for, he, the, to, was

Is it Late?   WORD COUNT: 111

DECODABLE WORDS
Target Phonics Elements
  Long *a, a_e:* ate, bakes, Blake,
  chase, date, game, grapes, Jane,
  Kate, late, make, plate, take, wake

HIGH-FREQUENCY WORDS
away, now, some, today, way,
why
Review: for, go, have, no, of,
place, she, the, to

A Fine Plant

DECODABLE WORDS
Target Phonics Elements
  Long *i, i_e:* Mike, fine, like, pine, rise,
  smile, time, vine, while

HIGH-FREQUENCY WORDS
green, grow, pretty, should,
together, water
Review: now, said, the

Plants Take Time to Grow   WORD COUNT: 120

DECODABLE WORDS
Target Phonics Elements
  Long *i, i_e:* fine, life, like, line, pine, pines,
  rise, shine, size, time

HIGH-FREQUENCY WORDS
green, grow, pretty, should,
together, water
Review: be, good, of, some, the,
they, to

King and Five Mice

DECODABLE WORDS
Target Phonics Elements
  Soft *c*, Soft *g*, *dge*; soft *c*: chance, face, mice, space; **soft *g*, *dge*:** budge, cage, edge, rage

HIGH-FREQUENCY WORDS
any, from, happy, once, so, upon
Review: green, of, out, said, the, to, was, way, we

Tales from a Past Age

DECODABLE WORDS
Target Phonics Elements
  Soft *c*, Soft *g*, *dge*; soft *c*: faces, mice, place, race; **soft *g*, *dge*:** age, ledge, bridge, cage, gem

HIGH-FREQUENCY WORDS
any, from, happy, once, so, upon
Review: are, go, have, of, look, the, they, two, way

Those Old Classes

DECODABLE WORDS
Target Phonics Elements
  Long *o*, *o_e*, Long *u*, *u_e*, Long *e*, *e_e*; long *o*: globe, lone, note, those, tone; **long *u*:** use, used, huge; **long *e*:** these

HIGH-FREQUENCY WORDS
ago, boy, girl, how, old, people
Review: could, for, from, have, one, many, now, school, the, they, to, today, was, you

---

That Old Globe

DECODABLE WORDS
Target Phonics Elements
  Long *o*, *o_e*, Long *u*, *u_e*, Long *e*, *e_e*; long *o*: globe, home, note, stove; **long *u*:** use, huge, mule; **long *e*:** Eve, Pete, these

HIGH-FREQUENCY WORDS
ago, boy, girl, how, old, people
Review: again, eat, from, now, of, said, the, there, they, to, was

A Good Cook   WORD COUNT: 138

DECODABLE WORDS
Target Phonics Elements
  Variant Vowel Spellings with Digraphs; *oo:* cook, food, good, hook, look; *u:* pull, push, put

HIGH-FREQUENCY WORDS
after, buy, done, every, soon, work
Review: be, he, help, of, people, she, the, too
Story Word: pizza

That Looks Good   WORD COUNT: 129

DECODABLE WORDS
Target Phonics Elements
  Variant Vowel Spellings with Digraphs; *oo:* cook, good, look, looks, took, wood; *u:* bull, pull

HIGH-FREQUENCY WORDS
after, buy, done, every, soon, work
Review: could, have, he, of, out, said, see, so, the, they, to, was, we, what

HIGH-FREQUENCY WORDS TAUGHT TO DATE

Kindergarten

a	too	every	school
and	want	from	should
are	was	fun	so
can	we	girl	some
come	what	good	soon
do	where	green	then
does	who	grow	there
for	with	happy	they
go	you	help	three
good		her	today
has	**Grade I**	how	together
have	after	jump	too
help	again	live	two
here	ago	make	under
I	all	many	up
is	any	move	upon
like	around	new	use
little	away	no	very
look	be	not	walk
me	boy	now	want
my	buy	of	water
of	by	old	way
play	call	once	what
said	come	one	who
see	could	out	why
she	day	people	work
the	does	place	
they	done	pretty	
this	down	pull	
to	eat	run	

DECODING SKILLS TAUGHT TO DATE

Short *a;* -s inflection endings; Short *i;* double final consonants; beginning consonant blends: *bl* blends, *cl* blends, *fl* blends, *gl* blends, *pl* blends, *sl* blends; *-s* (plural nouns); short *o;* alphabetical order (one letter); beginning consonant blends: *r*-blends; *s*-blends; possessives; short *e* spelled *e* and *ea;* inflection ending *-ed* (no spelling change); short *u;* contractions with *'s;* ending consonant blends *nd, nk, st, sk, mp;* inflection ending *ing* (no spelling change); consonant digraphs *th, sh, ng;* closed syllables; digraphs *ch, tch,* wh, *ph;* -es (plural nouns); long *a, a_e;* contractions with *not;* long *i, i_e;* plurals (with CVCe syllables); soft *c;* soft *g, dge;* -*ing* (drop the final *e*); long *o, o_e;* long *u, u_e;* long *e, e_e;* CVCe syllables; variant vowel spellings with digraphs: *oo, u;* inflection endings *-ed* and *-ing* (double final consonant)